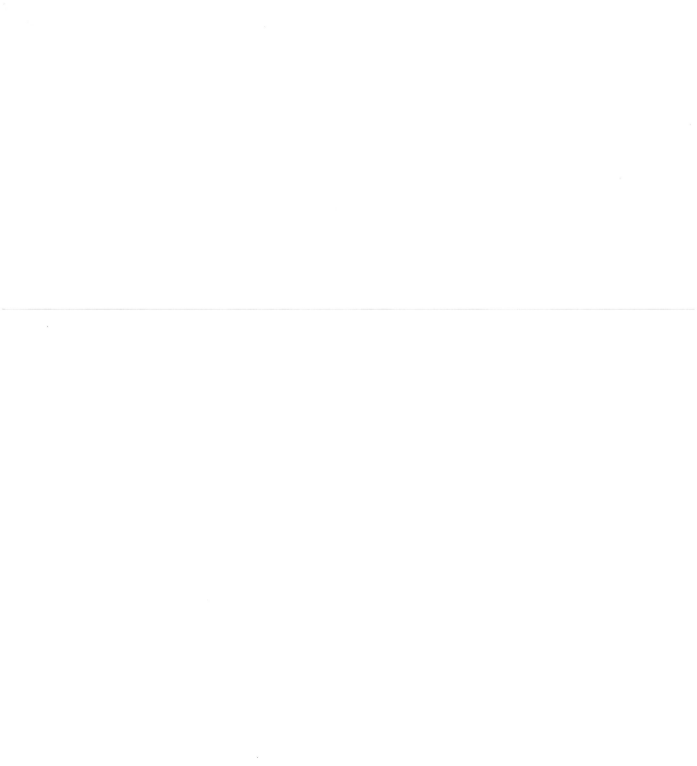

A DAY in the LIFE OF...

A NURSE

Written by Alex Hall

Published in 2025 by Enslow Publishing, LLC
2544 Clinton Street
Buffalo, NY 14224

© 2024 BookLife Publishing Ltd.

Written by:
Alex Hall

Edited by:
Rebecca Phillips-Bartlett

Designed by:
Amelia Harris

Cataloging-in-Publication Data

Names: Hall, Alex.
Title: A nurse / Alex Hall.
Description: Buffalo, NY : Enslow Publishing, 2025. | Series: A day in the life of… | Includes glossary and index.
Identifiers: ISBN 9781978541863 (pbk.) | ISBN 9781978541870 (library bound) | ISBN 9781978541887 (ebook)
Subjects: LCSH: Nurses--Juvenile literature.
Classification: LCC RT82.H355 2025 | DDC 610.73--dc23

All rights reserved.

No part of this book may be reproduced in any form without permission in writing from the publisher, except by a reviewer.

Manufactured in the United States of America

CPSIA compliance information: Batch #CW25ENS: For further information contact Enslow Publishing LLC at 1-800-398-2504.

Please visit our website, www.enslowpublishing.com. For a free color catalog of all our high-quality books, call toll free 1-800-398-2504 or fax 1-877-980-4454.

Find us on

Image Credits

All images are courtesy of Shutterstock.com, unless otherwise specified. With thanks to Getty Images, Thinkstock Photo and iStockphoto. Recurring – Lee Charlie, TWINS DESIGN STUDIO, RoseRodionova, Drazen Zigic, Studio Romantic, Vectors Bang, Amanita Silvicora. Cover – Studio Romantic, PedroNevesDesign. 2–3 – Nils Versemann. 4–5 – PeopleImages.com - Yuri A, Drazen Zigic. 6–7 – Wirestock Creators. 8–9 – oatawa, Ground Picture. 10–11 – Studio Romantic. 12–13 – RolandoE. 14–15 – Studio Romantic. 16–17 – Chay_Tee, alphabe. 18–19 – Nils Versemann, gpointstudio. 20–21 – fizkes, Owlie Productions. 22–23 – Studio Romantic.

CONTENTS

PAGE 4 A Day in the Life
PAGE 6 Different Nurses, Different Places
PAGE 8 Starting the Day
PAGE 10 Checking Patients
PAGE 12 Giving Medication
PAGE 14 Educating Patients
PAGE 16 Helping People
PAGE 18 Emergency!
PAGE 20 Writing the Daily Report
PAGE 22 Would You Like to Be a Nurse?
PAGE 24 Glossary and Index

Words that look like this can be found in the glossary on page 24.

A Day in the Life

There are so many different jobs that you could do when you get older. Different jobs need different skills. Do you know what job you want to do when you are older?

Chef

Police officer

Most jobs need special skills and knowledge. A nurse is someone who cares for people who are ill and need help. A nurse needs to know a lot about health.

DIFFERENT NURSES, DIFFERENT PLACES

Different types of nurses work in different places. Nurses work in hospitals, walk-in clinics, and emergency transportation. Some nurses work in schools to help children who feel ill.

Ambulance

Does your school have a nurse?

Some nurses work in nursing homes. Nursing homes are places where older people live when they cannot look after themselves. No matter where they work, all nurses care for people.

7

STARTING THE DAY

Some nurses start their day early in the morning. Some nurses work at night and come home in the morning. This makes sure a nurse is always there to care for patients.

When a nurse arrives at work, they read a report about their patients. The nurse from the last <u>shift</u> wrote the report. The report tells the nurse everything they need to know about their patients.

Sharing the report is called a handover.

CHECKING PATIENTS

The next part of a nurse's day is to check on their patients. A nurse checks their patient to see whether they are better or worse. They do this by looking at their symptoms.

Symptoms are things that our bodies do to show us that we are not well. A nurse is often the first person to notice any issues and help stop them from getting worse.

Nurses may use *equipment* to help them.

GIVING MEDICATION

Some people who are ill need medication. Nurses are often responsible for giving patients their medication. Nurses need to fill out forms to track what medicines have been given.

Nurses use math to figure out how much medicine they need to give and at what time they need to give it. It can be dangerous if they give the patient too much medication.

13

EDUCATING PATIENTS

Nurses educate their patients and their loved ones about their illness. This helps the patient understand what is happening to them, how they might feel, and how they can help themselves feel better.

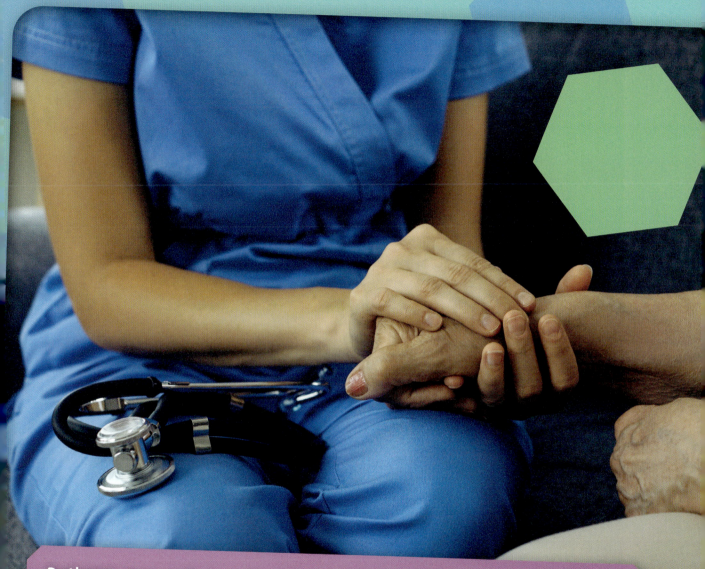

Patients may ask questions, and the nurse will answer as many as they can. Patients might be upset, and the nurse will comfort them. Nurses need to be clear and calm when talking to patients.

HELPING PEOPLE

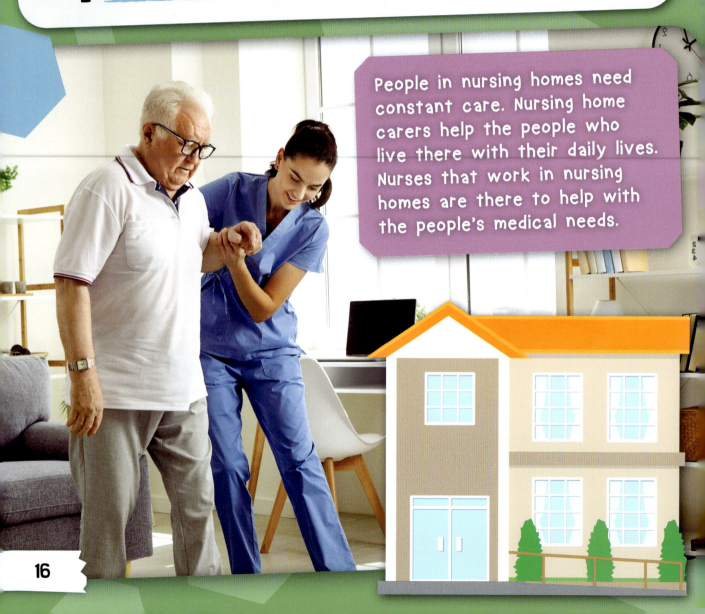

People in nursing homes need constant care. Nursing home carers help the people who live there with their daily lives. Nurses that work in nursing homes are there to help with the people's medical needs.

Nurses create care plans with the nursing home carers. These plans will explain how to take care of the patients. The plan might have important notes about how and when to give medication.

17

EMERGENCY!

Sometimes, patients will get ill or injured very suddenly and need extra care. This is called an emergency. Nurses will often be the first people to arrive to help.

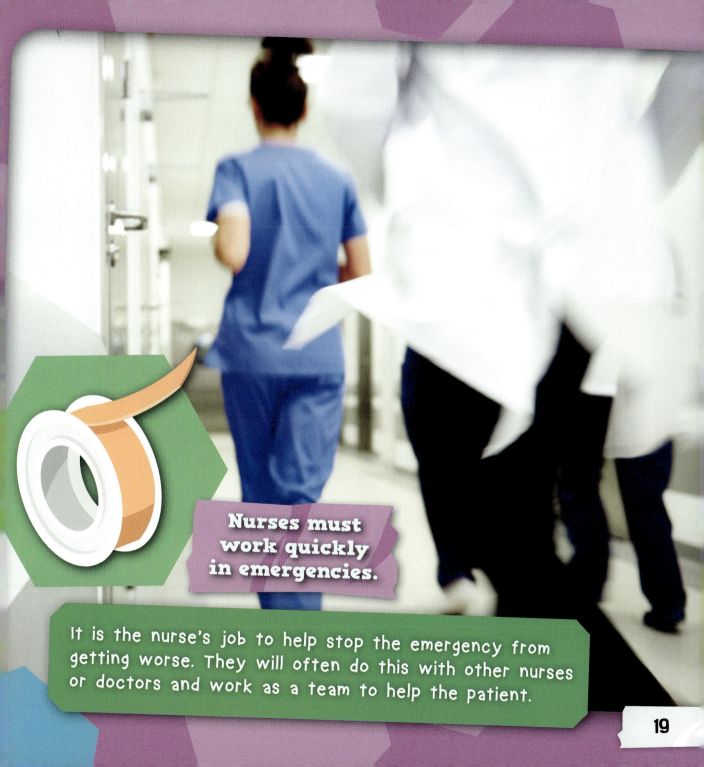

Nurses must work quickly in emergencies.

It is the nurse's job to help stop the emergency from getting worse. They will often do this with other nurses or doctors and work as a team to help the patient.

Writing the Daily Report

Nurses finish the day by writing a daily report. Nurses make sure everything about their patients is noted in the report. It is important that everything in the report is correct.

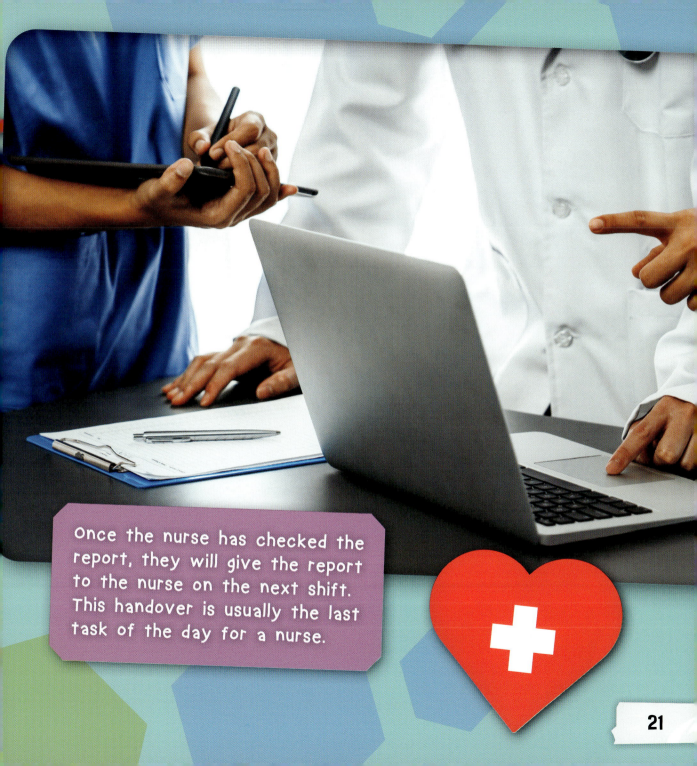

Once the nurse has checked the report, they will give the report to the nurse on the next shift. This handover is usually the last task of the day for a nurse.

WOULD YOU LIKE TO BE A NURSE?

You need to learn a lot about medicine and the human body to be a nurse. You also need to be kind to your patients to help them stay calm when they are still ill.

Being a nurse is hard work, but it is also very rewarding. Helping someone feel better may make you happy too.

Do you think that you could be a nurse one day?

GLOSSARY

EDUCATE	to teach someone
EQUIPMENT	items that are needed to complete a certain job
INJURED	when someone has been harmed or damaged by someone or something
MEDICATION	drugs that are used to treat pain and illness
PATIENTS	people who are given medical care or treatment
RESPONSIBLE	in charge of doing certain things
SHIFT	the set amount of time that a group works for before handing over to another group to do the same job
TRANSPORTATION	something that can get someone from one place to another

BODIES 11, 22
DOCTORS 19
EMERGENCIES 6, 18–19
FORMS 12
HOSPITALS 6
NURSING HOMES 7, 16–17
REPORTS 9, 20–21
SCHOOLS 6
SHIFTS 9, 21
SYMPTOMS 10–11
WALK-IN CLINICS 6

24